Moses And Deuteronomy

Samuel Ives Curtiss Jr.

In the interest of creating a more extensive selection of rare historical book reprints, we have chosen to reproduce this title even though it may possibly have occasional imperfections such as missing and blurred pages, missing text, poor pictures, markings, dark backgrounds and other reproduction issues beyond our control. Because this work is culturally important, we have made it available as a part of our commitment to protecting, preserving and promoting the world's literature. Thank you for your understanding.

MOSES AND DEUTERONOMY.

No. 3 OF THE "PRESENT DAY PAPERS"
From the "Family Treasury," March 1878.

BY

SAMUEL IVES CURTISS, JUN.,
Author of "The Levitical Priests."

LONDON: THOMAS NELSON AND SONS.
EDINBURGH AND NEW YORK.
1878.

TO

𝔐𝔶 𝔅𝔢𝔩𝔬𝔳𝔢𝔡 𝔗𝔢𝔞𝔠𝔥𝔢𝔯,

REV. JULIUS H. SEELYE, D.D. LL.D.,
President of Amherst College, Mass., U.S.A.,

IN

GRATEFUL RECOGNITION.

Contents.

I. PASSAGES CONTAINING POST-MOSAIC REFERENCES 7
II. POST-MOSAIC LAWS 14
III. REFERENCES TO DEUTERONOMY BY THE PROPHETS OF THE EIGHTH CENTURY 22
IV. ARGUMENTS IN FAVOUR OF THE MOSAIC AUTHORSHIP 24
V. POSITION OF GERMAN EVANGELICAL CRITICS 29

MOSES AND DEUTERONOMY.

CHAPTER I.

PASSAGES CONTAINING POST-MOSAIC REFERENCES.

T is the almost unanimous verdict of modern criticism that Deuteronomy was written about the time of Manasseh or Josiah. The critics affirm that the object of the writer was to promote unity in the worship of Jehovah, as well as purity in public and private life. The Deuteronomist, that he may secure these reforms, makes the most honoured name in all Jewish history—that of Moses—the bearer of his message to his countrymen; or rather, he makes Moses speak as he would have done had he been living. To hold, on the Continent, that Deuteronomy was composed before Manasseh or Josiah, is to expose

oneself to the charge of an unscientific spirit, and a dogmatism which renders a man deaf to every sound argument.

While I do not fear the ostracism of scientific opinion, yet I wish honestly to recognize the full force of the critical arguments. Let us then briefly examine some of the reasons why the critics would have us believe that Deuteronomy was not written until centuries after Moses. These are mainly threefold: (1) Certain expressions which Moses could not have used; (2) certain laws, whose origin must be assigned to a much later period than that of the great lawgiver; (3) the absence of allusions to this book by the prophets of the eighth century. Of course there are several other grounds which are of subordinate importance, and for which there is no room in a brief and popular article.

If we look carefully at the passages which are alleged to contain post-Mosaic references, we shall find that they are either parenthetical or additional; so that if we were to admit that they were un-Mosaic, it would by no means follow that the book in which they occur could not be from Moses, any more than an edition of a classic author ceases to be genuine because explanatory notes have been inserted. As a general thing, however, it is not necessary to admit that the passages in question are parenthetical. It is said that the expression—"These be the words which Moses spake unto Israel on this side [more accurately, *on the other side*] Jordan" (i. 1)—indicates that the author was living in the land of Canaan. This really affords no difficulty, since Moses could hardly have written otherwise in a book which he intended for Israel after the conquest (xxxi. 10).

Special emphasis is put upon the words: "The Horim formerly dwelt in Seir; but the children of Esau drove them out, and destroyed them before them; *as Israel did to the land of his possession, which Jehovah gave him*" (ii. 12). This is regarded as a slip on the part of the Deuteronomist, and as indicating that Israel had long been in possession of the promised land. Although this reading is sustained by the Septuagint and the Massorah, I am inclined to think that, after the analogy of an oft repeated formula (iv. 40; ix. 6, &c.), it originally read: "As Israel *is doing* to the land of his possession which Jehovah *is giving* him." If any are not satisfied with this solution, which seems to me to be perfectly legitimate, and which, as I have since found, was adopted by Vogel in his edition of Grotius, still all difficulty disappears when we consider that the Deuteronomist regards the conquest and possession of Canaan as a foregone conclusion, of which the victories on the east side of Jordan are the pledges. He frequently speaks of Israel as in the act of crossing the Jordan (iv. 26; xi. 31; xxxi. 13, *you are crossing the Jordan*), and of the land which the Lord is giving them (iv. 1; v. 16, &c.), or has given them (viii. 10; xii. 1). Hence there would have been no inconsistency, in view of the victories over the Amorites on the east side of the Jordan, in Moses writing of that which had been so successfully begun, and which he knew would be successfully accomplished—" As Israel did unto the land of his possession which the Lord gave unto him." Besides, it was perfectly in keeping for the speaker to say Israel instead of Reuben, Gad, and the half tribe of Manasseh (iv. 47; compare ver. 45).

Og's bedstead* (iii. 11), although long enough, has been made the most of by the critics. They claim that it is mentioned as an antiquity, and is designed to substantiate the writer's statement in regard to the immense height of Og. This by no means follows. The writer alludes in confirmation of the great victory over the giant king to a bedstead in Rabbath, of which he gives the exact dimensions. This fact was interesting, not only for those for whom the book was immediately designed, but also for their descendants. A verse, however, almost immediately follows, which I feel constrained to yield to the critics, and that is where Jair is said to have taken all

---

* I have not been misled in this case by the English version, as the reviewer of "The Levitical Priests" in the *Scotsman* might suppose. Knobel admits that bedstead is a better translation, but prefers sarcophagus, because he thinks that otherwise Og would have been too tall.

the region of Argob, and to have called it Bashan, after his name,—villages of Jair unto this day (iii. 14). While the expression, "unto this day," often merely means *until now* (Joshua xxiii. 8, 9), and is used as the boundary of a brief period (*ten years*, Jer. xxv. 3; *a few months*, 1 Sam. xxix. 3; xxvii. 7), yet it does not seem probable that Moses could have used this language of an event which only took place about three months before. As I have already said, the assignment of this parenthetical remark to a subsequent period would not invalidate the Mosaic authorship of Deuteronomy.

The last three chapters of Deuteronomy, which contain directions as to the place where the book of the law is to be kept (xxxi. 26), and the account of Moses' death, need afford no difficulty. Thoroughly Deuteronomic in character, they could have been added by some disciple of Moses. The critics, indeed, claim that the closing verses indicate that they were written ages after the death of Moses. But when we carefully examine them, we find that this is not the case. The words, "No man knoweth of his sepulchre unto this day" (xxxiv. 6), probably indicate a few years rather than several centuries, since they seem to show that the Israelites searched in vain for the burial-place of Moses, as the sons of the prophets sent a company to look for Elijah (2 Kings ii. 16, 17) after his translation. The assertion in xxxiv. 10 might seem to indicate, as the critics claim, that it was written as late as the reign of Josiah. If, however, we translate the verse, "And there has not yet arisen a prophet in Israel like unto Moses," &c., the difficulty is removed, and at the same time the disappointment of the generation following the great lawgiver at the non-fulfilment of the promise in xviii. 15, 18 is clearly indicated.

CHAPTER II.

POST-MOSAIC LAWS.

PASS now to consider certain laws, whose origin, according to the critics, must be assigned to a much later period than that of the great lawgiver. These laws are in reference to a central sanctuary, the tribe of Levi, and the king. The critics affirm that in every passage where mention is made of the place which the Lord will choose to set his name there (xii. 5, 11, &c.) Jerusalem is designated. The writer is said to have been moved to this by witnessing the evils which were occasioned by the worship on the high places. Probably none will deny that Moses might expect that the Lord would choose a city out of all the tribes as the place for his sanctuary. Here, however, the critics say, Is it not strange that so many godly men for centuries, as Samuel and others, should have

disregarded the command, "Take heed to thyself that thou offer not burnt offerings in every place that thou seest"? (xii. 13). I do not see any difficulty here. We read in so many words that the Lord had no settled sanctuary until the building of the temple at Jerusalem. This is sufficient excuse for the action of all persons previous to the time of Solomon (1 Kings viii. 16; 2 Sam. vii. 6; 1 Kings iii. 2). When we consider, too, how many statutes become obsolete through ages of disregard, it need not surprise us that the example of so many good men should have deadened the public conscience with respect to this law, and robbed it of its force.

In respect to the tribe of Levi, it is affirmed that, while the middle books of the Pentateuch sharply distinguish between the members of that tribe, the priests and the Levites, the book of Deuteronomy does not recognize any such distinction. Its priests are Levites, or sons of Levi. No barriers exist within the tribe against those who desire admission to the priesthood. The endowment, however, of the tribe with these sacerdotal privileges is attended, according to one school of critics (Riehm), with a serious diminution of income, through the changes which have been introduced by the Deuteronomist with reference to the tithes. The other school of critics (Graf), however, simply regards the Levitical priests as a certain grade in a process of development, which culminates in the Aaronitic priesthood.

Into this question, which I have fully discussed in another place,* I can here only very briefly enter. It must not be forgotten that the Deuteronomist represents Moses as delivering an address to the people. If the code in the preceding books was substantially in existence, there would be no occasion for the lawgiver to repeat it, to say nothing of the specific laws as being out of the range of the common people. Supposing that it was the purpose of the writer to introduce a modified legislation in regard to the tribe of Levi, to break down the old barriers which excluded all who were not sons of Aaron

---

* "The Levitical Priests." T. and T. Clark, Edinburgh. 1877.

from the priesthood, we can only wonder that so important a change should have been ushered in by means of these scattered utterances. If, however, we accept Graf's and Kuenen's theory, that the Levitical priests are part of a development, it seems still more strange that we should have so little in regard to so important a regulation. Looking at the matter now from the ordinary standpoint, that Moses. was addressing Israel as a whole, composed of twelve tribes, it does not seem surprising that he should designate the priests after their tribe as Levites (xvii. 9, 18; xviii. 1; xxiv. 8; xxvii. 9), or sons of Levi (xxxi. 9), or that he should speak of their duties (x. 8) and privileges (xviii. 1–8) as a tribe, rather than as two classes making up the tribe.

If we regard the laws in reference to the tithes in Deuteronomy (xii. 17, 18; xiv. 22–29) as the abrogation of those in the preceding books, it seems very remarkable that no allusion whatever should have been made to the previous laws (Num. xviii.). If, however, we see in these passages the duties of the people in regard to certain festivals, the exhortations and commands seem natural enough; and, as I have shown in my "Levitical Priests," the tithes in Deuteronomy do not abrogate those in the preceding books. At the same time, the exhortations to remember the Levite (xiv. 27), and the designation of the priest's due from the people at their slaughterings* (xviii. 3), no more exclude their regular income, than a charge to the people of a country parish to remember their minister and give the usual presents would indicate a release from the stipulated salary. There seems, then, to be nothing in these references to the Levitical priests which renders the Mosaic authorship of Deuteronomy impossible or improbable.

It is affirmed, however, that the law in regard to the king (xvii. 15–20; comp. xxviii. 36) indicates a period long subsequent to Solomon. The command that he should not multiply wives to himself, is said to have been written with direct reference to Solomon's sad experience;

---

* See "The Levitical Priests," pp. 41–45.

and the command that he shall not multiply horses to himself, nor cause the people to return to Egypt to the end that he should multiply horses, clearly indicates, according to Ewald and Riehm, that this book was written in the time of Manasseh. Riehm does not deny that Moses might foresee such an event as the choice of a king, but he thinks it incredible that such a regulation could have been in existence in the time of Gideon and Samuel. How, say the critics, could Gideon have refused to rule over Israel, and have said, " The Lord shall rule over you " (Judges viii. 22, 23), if he had known these words? Undoubtedly there was a strong feeling among the more devout, including Gideon, that God was the King of Israel. His apparent ignorance of these words is no proof that they did not then exist, but it is rather probable that in those times of gross apostasy Deuteronomy was no longer read to the people (Deut. xxxi. 11). The objection is urged, that it is strange that no mention was made of this law by the people who came to Samuel. But the fact that what took place is reported in outline rather than in detail, is a sufficient answer. Besides, the people show Samuel, almost in the very language of the passage in Deuteronomy, that it is their wish that a king should be set over them (comp. 1 Sam. viii. 5 with Deut. xvii. 14). Although he had made his sons judges over Israel (1 Sam. viii. 1), he evidently regards the proposition as a personal affront. This is clear from the language with which God comforts him—"They have not rejected thee, but they have rejected me" (1 Sam. viii. 7). These cases, therefore, viewed in this light, cannot disprove the existence of this law in the time of Gideon and Samuel.

Ewald has constructed out of this passage in connection with xxviii. 68 a plausible theory, in which he claims that Manasseh transported Israelites to Egypt to obtain horses from King Psammetich. This theory is more ingenious than probable, and is without any direct historical support. How much such warnings as those in the above verses were needed, appears from the occasional longings of the Israelites for Egypt, even in the time of Moses, and also from the words of the prophets. Zedekiah, indeed, did rebel against Nebuchadnezzar (2 Kings xxiv. 20), and sought an alliance with Egypt, and horses and troops thereby (Ezek. xvii. 15). After the plot had been discovered, and the king and many of the people carried into captivity, and after Gedaliah had been slain, Johanan, who had charge of the remnant, took them to Egypt (Jer. xli. 16; xliii. 7). Whether this transportation was effected by means of ships cannot now be determined. They assembled at Bethlehem (Jer. xli. 17), and from this point might have gone to one of the old sea-ports of Dan or Asher (Judges v. 17), instead of taking the long and trying overland route.

When, therefore, we consider the history of Israel as a whole, and Moses' knowledge of the people, not to speak of his prophetic insight, there seems no difficulty in supposing that he foresaw that they would demand a king, and that he provided for this exigency in accordance with the divine plan.

CHAPTER III.

REFERENCES TO DEUTERONOMY BY THE PROPHETS OF THE EIGHTH CENTURY.

PERHAPS one of the weakest points which the critics have made, is what they call the total absence from the prophets of the eighth century of any allusions to Deuteronomy, while Jeremiah abounds in them. It certainly is not strange that Jeremiah was saturated with a book which was found while he was a young man (Jer. i. 2, 6, 7; 2 Kings xxii. 3-8), and which made such a profound impression upon the king and people. We have no means of determining how long the book of the law had been lost, or whether it had been read every seven years to the people. It is not probable that the prophets of the eighth century had free access to it; still I am confident that it cannot be proved that these prophets do not betray any knowledge of the Deuteronomic law. Their style has not been moulded by it; and yet Hosea (v. 10) uses an expression, when he says that Ephraim shall be like *them which remove the bound*, which (as a participle *) is only found here and in Deuteronomy xix. 14; xxvii. 17. The threatening that the people shall return to Egypt (viii. 13; ix. 3) reminds us of Deuteronomy xxviii. 68; and the words, "I did know thee in the wilderness, in the land of great drought" (xiii. 5), seem to be in allusion to Deuteronomy ii. 7; viii. 15). While I might quote several other passages indicating that Hosea, Joel, and Amos had at least some acquaintance with Deuteronomy, and how much Isaiah † has borrowed from it, I cannot, within the limits of this article, give more extended proof. It seems to me, however, that the assertion that Deuteronomy was not known to the prophets of the eighth century cannot stand.

---

* The future is found in Proverbs xxii. 28; xxiii. 10.
† See Delitzsch's *Commentar über die Genesis* (Leipzig, 1872), s. 10.

CHAPTER IV.

ARGUMENTS IN FAVOUR OF THE MOSAIC AUTHORSHIP.

T is not only possible to answer every objection against the Mosaic authorship of Deuteronomy, but also to show that it is highly improbable that the book of Deuteronomy, taken as a whole, should have been written in the time of Manasseh or Josiah,—or, indeed, at any very long remove from the death of Moses.

If we look at the first three chapters of the book, in which Moses is represented as giving a historical retrospect of events which he and his hearers have witnessed, the question arises, What object could a writer in the time of Manasseh have had in rehearsing these events, even if we could suppose him capable of so doing? Why should he speak of the wonderful deliverance which Israel, as children, had witnessed on the shores of the Red Sea? Why should he remind them that they were bondsmen in Egypt, if the story of their parents' sufferings were not sufficiently fresh to make them sympathize with slaves and strangers? (v. 15; xv. 15; xxiv. 18.) What object would there be in the allusions to Egypt, unless the speaker and people had recently come from it? They receive the promise that, if obedient, they shall not suffer from any of the diseases of Egypt (vii. 15); and that they shall inherit a land of hills and valleys watered from heaven, which they will not need to irrigate with their foot (xi. 10). Many of the directions given are with reference to the conquest of Canaan. They are not to fear the nations which they are about to displace, and which the Lord will drive out gradually (vii. 16-23). They are to utterly destroy Amalek (xxv. 19). Are we, then, to suppose that this was a matter of such importance in the time of Manasseh as to be so especially mentioned? The regulation regarding the marriage of an Israelite with a beautiful captive (xxi. 10-14) is entirely in place in the days of the conquest; but it seems rather far-fetched in the time of Manasseh, when the cruel king was selling the Israelites to Egypt for horses, as Ewald would have us believe. Can we suppose that the Deuteronomist writing at that time would make such a regulation, or that he would give such minute regulations for the cleanliness of the Israelitic camp as we find in Deuteronomy xxiii. 12-14?

Then, again, there are numerous laws which have no special application to any one time in the history of Israel, which cannot be made exclusively appropriate to the time of Manasseh or Josiah without violence. It is not difficult to find in Deuteronomy directions for Israel from the very moment of its crossing the Jordan to the latest times of its ancient history. But it would require a frequent use of the critic's scissors to construct a book which could with special fitness be addressed to Manasseh or Josiah and their contemporaries.

In harmony with the testimony which the book bears on its very face, is the explicit statement in Deuteronomy xxxi. 9, 24, that Moses wrote this book. It may be asserted that these verses do not definitely indicate Deuteronomy. Such an objection, however, is a mere quibble. When we consider the essential unity of Deuteronomy, which all critics admit, we must understand them as referring to the book in hand. The critics rightly contend that they (xxxi. 9, 24) could not have been written by Moses; but when they affirm, as Bleek does, that if they are not from Moses they are of no value, I cannot assent, since, as we have seen, there is nothing to prevent our supposing that they were written not very long after the death of Moses. In any case, they merely confirm the internal evidence of the book in regard to itself.

We are driven, therefore, to the conclusion, either that Deuteronomy, essentially as it now stands, was spoken and written by Moses, or that it was composed in the period of Manasseh-Josiah; and that the author, that he might render the Mosaic character of the book as strong as possible, made the scenery, the history, and the laws of the early Israelites so prominent, as to be out of all proportion to those special lessons which were necessary for a particular period, and on account of which, as the critics affirm, the book was written. Is the latter supposition credible? Could any prophet in the time of Manasseh or Josiah have written as the Deuteronomist has done?

It seems to me that to any unprejudiced mind these considerations are sufficient, and I would feel satisfied to rest the case here, so far as the proof is concerned. The fact that I consider another point is not because I feel the need of any dogmatic arguments in support of my position, for I am convinced on critical grounds that Moses was the author of Deuteronomy. There would, however, be no special use in arguing the question, if it did not involve principles of the greatest importance, not only in our views of the origin and authority of the Old Testament, but also of the New.

CHAPTER V.

POSITION OF GERMAN EVANGELICAL CRITICS.

VANGELICAL critics naturally shrink from the conclusion that if Deuteronomy is not from Moses, it is a pious fraud. Ewald, who in comparison with many critics must be called devout, uses all his dramatic power to show how an exiled prophet felt compelled to use the last resource, and announce his message in the name of Moses rather than through a "Thus saith the Lord." Riehm claims that we must not judge him according to the New Testament standard of morality. Others have sought to excuse him by saying that he has merely adopted a form of composition then common, such as we find in the titles of certain Psalms and in Ecclesiastes. The cases, however, are not parallel, for there is not only the announcement in Deuteronomy that Moses was its author, but the greatest effort in the choice of the occasion, and in the whole cast of the book, down to

the minutest details, to produce this impression. Now, when Kuenen implies that this book is a pious fraud, he is consistent with himself, and is completely emancipated from theological influences; while Bleek, Ewald, and Riehm have not been able fully to overcome dogmatic prejudices. The only consistent position is either to hold that Deuteronomy is from Moses, or that it is a pious fraud. To adopt the critical views of Bleek and others, is to be compelled by every canon of criticism and the stern logic of present events to the latter position. What then? The course of criticism has shown that the same flood which has swept away the Mosaic authorship of Deuteronomy can undermine the authority of John's Gospel. The same strict scientific method which affirms as axiomatic that Deuteronomy was written in the time of Josiah, can raise the queries: Is there any scientific proof that Jesus was not born of natural parents; that his resurrection and ascension are not a fiction of his disciples; that the doctrine of his divinity is not the invention of some sect? Certainly, if Deuteronomy is a pious fraud, the Gospels may be. If the Holy Ghost can make such means the channels of his communication, then we experience great moral confusion, and we give the enemies of revealed religion a great advantage.

It is idle to quote great names in a discussion of this kind. Great learning is sometimes accompanied with intellectual obtuseness, not to say prejudice and pride of opinion.

The positions of the critics have been subject to many changes. Bleek died (1859) before the new school was ushered in (by Graf, 1866). Even such a "sincere believer in the Word of God" as Kamphausen (Candlish), considers Bleek in some points as much too conservative. Ewald (died 1875) treated the new school with haughty indifference. Riehm, one of the most devout of the critics, has manifested signs of wavering in his views, which he put forth in 1854, and has made some important concessions to the new school (Graf, Nöldeke). The argument then that a man may hold these critical views and still be a pillar of orthodoxy, in view of the latest developments of the critical school in Germany, is not to the purpose. A man's heart may be right, although his theories are very injurious. Doubtless every sincere Christian feels that, should criticism do its worst, he would still cling to the Rock of Ages. This, however, should not render us indifferent to the subversive tendency of some critical opinions.

There can be but one position for the Church. It is that of perfect trust in Him who hath said, "I am the way, the truth, and the life." If there should not be undue haste in affirming that only the Mosaic authorship is possible, how much care should be taken against adopting and disseminating destructive critical views. They should be tested with the same scientific diligence by devout scholars in Great Britain and America, which has been applied to the Bible in Germany, where in most learned circles it would be considered arrant heresy to believe in the Mosaic authorship of Deuteronomy. Here we can afford to make haste slowly, and to be but little in the world's esteem, asking Him who is the light to illuminate our minds unto the knowledge of his truth.

[The End.]

Printed by Libri Plureos GmbH in Hamburg, Germany